SWAMP STORY

An Allegorical Tale

Jeffrey E. Reeves BA, MA, EUREKONOMIST™

The Courageous Escape from the Heart of the Financial Swamp

An allegorical tale about mosquitoes, alligators, snakes, sharks, storm, wave, raging-river, and dragonfly.

Discover if you are one of the human denizens of the Financial Swamp that may never escape because you have no guide or because your guide is dazed, confused, or lost.

Table of Contents

INTRODUCTION

The Courageous Escape from the Heart of the Financial Swamp

    I. The Awakening

    II. The Journey

    III. The Quest

    IV. The Treasure

EPILOGUE

Appendix A

INTRODUCTION

"If you do what everyone else does, you'll get the same results they do."
    Dr Agon Fly

The brightest and best minds in the *investment* community managed huge *mutual fund portfolios* during the disastrous post 9/11/2001 *bear market* and again in the financial and economic crisis of 2007 – 2008, **and they all lost**.

It was easy for them to look like geniuses during the *bull market* of the '90's. Everything from the *Pollyanna complacency* of the Clinton administration, to the apparent well-being of the world, to "dot.com fever," to the *grotesque* dishonesty of ENRON, MCI and other *self-aggrandizing* executives and market traders deceived us all into a false sense of security regarding the pure *unrelenting* risk of owning investments you don't control.

However, when the *ethereal economy* of those years crashed at the same time the World Trade Center Towers came down and when the *palpable* failure of the entire *paradigm* took place in the past few years, we all had to look at the *stark* reality of our world through a different set of lenses. It became clear that the *gurus* were not so smart and the paradigm that we relied on was flawed beyond our wildest imagination.

This is a wake-up call. Americans must realize that the financial thinking, planning, and practices we relied on during the last half of the 20th century are – simply stated – completely wrong.

- It is wrong to think that your economic future could be directly tied to the *market* and still offer safety,
- It is wrong to base our plans for our future security on *fickle*, *volatile* investments, and the *incessant* reuse of *home equity*, while we ignore with *disdain* the financial products that promise a much

higher lever of security and significant long-term growth;
- It is wrong to follow a practice where the bulk of our wealth is *vested* in high-risk investments that rely on tax-advantage for their *viability*
  - that some future administration of the Federal Government can *ultimately manipulate* without our consent,
  - that might diminish in value, and
  - that offer no guarantees.

·····

The SWAMP STORY is an allegory designed to help us see the *fallacies* of this *outmoded* paradigm and get a glimpse of a new model for personal financial behavior based on solid economic principles. The uniqueness of this new way of dealing with money is that it relies on **preparation instead of planning.**

Let me explain.

The biggest *myth* about personal finances is that we can effectively write a *financial plan* that is reliable, *executable*, and *predictable*. Remember September 10th, 2001? Probably not, but you likely knew nothing about the pending disaster and had no plans in place to deal with it. No one could predict 9/11/2001, much less 9/11/2002 or 2012 or 2022. Would you like to predict 9/11/2025 and have your family rely on that? Perhaps execute their plans based on it? I would expect not.

On the other hand, would you be willing to adopt an approach that dealt not with outcomes – the totally unpredictable – but with *expectations*, *probabilities*, and *possibilities*; in other words, preparations. That's what our government is doing about terrorism. That's what we need to do about our money. Let's try an analogy.

If you were preparing to build a house, you would first draw up plans. Now, if your plan was not designed for a specific lot you would surely have to either find a lot that suited those plans or modify the plans after you had chosen the lot.

As you begin digging the foundation, you might find the earth on the lot contains pockets of quicksand that need to be solidified, or that there are huge boulders below the surface that needed to be removed entirely from the location before you proceed. You may also discover that the dimensions of the lot require that the building be reoriented to satisfy local setback requirements.[1]

And so it will go throughout the building process: move a door slightly, then remove a wall to expand the bath, then change the fixtures in the kitchen because the cabinets' colors have been changed. None of this is planned, but somehow it all gets done and the house ends up just the way you wanted it. Why? Because the plans themselves were not the result;

---

[1] These are not exaggerated possibilities. I have personal experience with each of these situations.

they were only a guide. They are the map not the territory. The success of the house-building project is not the result of the plans. It results from the *preparedness* of the people who execute the plan and their ability to *adapt* to ever-changing conditions and situations.

Your personal economy is like the house. It is first an idea or set of ideas that you want to convert into practices that will *ultimately* create the kind of personal economy that will sustain you and your family. To think that someone could, in fact, write a plan for you that would turn out precisely the way it was written is just as foolhardy as expecting the *tangible* house to look exactly like the two-dimensional drawing. In order for the plan to work the way you want it to, *you* must execute it with all the same *aplomb* as the carpenter who adjusts to the *warp* of the wood, or the plumber who adapts to dimensional differences.

There is an obvious difference between the *analogy* and the reality. You may feel that a licensed and/or registered financial advisor is responsible for executing your plan. Just as the builder does the day-to-day work on the house, you expect the advisor to write mortgages, buy, and sell securities, identify college-funding opportunities, calculate your life insurance needs, recommend investments, and so on. That is where the analogy fails. Your builder is under contract to produce something specific and is responsible to you for doing so. *You are the only person responsible for your personal and family economy.* A financial advisor is insulated from that responsibility by the compliance department of his firm, whose main *raison d'être* is to make sure that your advisor doesn't do or say anything that could be construed as accepting any responsibility for your personal economy or for the outcome of your financial decisions.

"What's the alternative?" you might ask.

The alternative is to adopt the *EUREKONOMICS*™ model. This approach has been tested and proven for over a century. It allows you to use the expertise and skills of those in the financial community without relying on the advisor to take responsibility for your outcomes. In most cases these advisors are restrained by the laws that regulate their industry and also by the firms they represent.

This may seem a daunting challenge. You may feel that you are not equipped to act on your own behalf or that you do not have enough information to begin such an undertaking. You will be surprised to know that, even if you have no financial background, the *EUREKONOMICS™ Model for wealth Creation and Money Management* allows you to make informed and effective decisions that are in direct alignment with your personal economic goals.

Understanding this approach to personal economy is the entire and only objective of this brief allegory. So let's get started.

The Courageous Escape from the Heart of the Financial Swamp

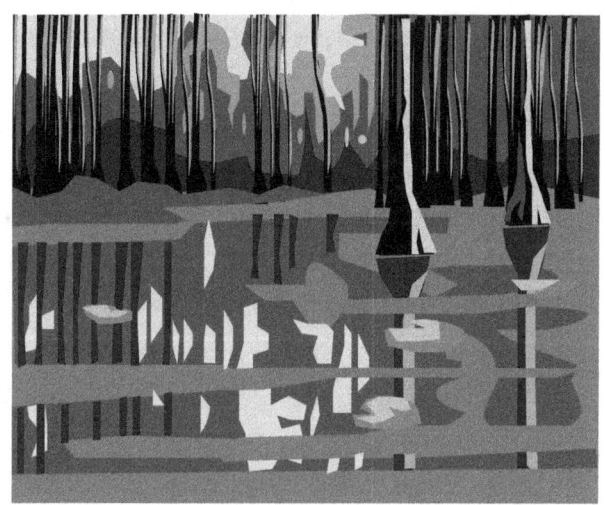

I. The Awakening

Call me dragonfly. I am going to tell you the story of Geo.

Geo lived in the deepest and darkest place: the Heart of the Swamp. When I met Geo he was just a lad. Geo was a clear thinking, hard-working youth and, like many of his peers, never had an inclination that there might be a place better than the place where he was born and raised. He saw the sun through the overburden of foliage that entombed the Heart of the Swamp and was always grateful for its scattered droplets of warmth and light. He never considered that there might be a world where the sun's full brilliance could be seen and embraced; where the night sky was more than the occasional flicker of a star, or the dappled light of the moon that periodically graced nighttime in the Heart of the Swamp.

Geo waded on the muddy bottom of the Heart of the Swamp during the day as he worked diligently at his trade and he rested peacefully in the arms of one of her many trees at night. He was careful to avoid the Alligator and Snake

who were his cohabitants. He relished the pleasures of the Heart of the Swamp's many delicacies and he had me, dragonfly, to eat the mosquitoes that were constantly circling to find an exposed bit of flesh where they could land to extract their drop of blood. Although dragonfly has been in the Heart of the Swamp for over 300,000,000[2] years and has eaten trillions of mosquitoes, the mosquitoes keep coming back. Some almost

---

[2] The dragonfly is one of the oldest creatures on Earth and is said to have had a wingspan of over 20 feet when it flew the primordial skies over 300 million years ago. Perhaps the reason dragonfly has survived is because he deals with a persistent pest.

always get past dragonfly and greedily engorge themselves.

So it was with Geo, but he didn't seem to mind too much. That's just the way it is in the Heart of the Swamp, and everyone just puts up with it. In fact, if you complain about the mosquitoes the PC Police[3] remind you that the mosquitoes have all the same rights as you. They emphasize that balance in the Heart of the Swamp depends on everyone playing their role; that your role is to give up a drop of blood

---

[3] PC = Politically Correct; yes, even in the Heart of the Swamp.

whenever you must, and that your attitude needs adjustment.

Geo was happy and content in the Heart of the Swamp until the fateful day his best friend, Able, was pulled under the murky waters of the Heart of the Swamp by Alligator, and never came back up.

Able had been so engrossed in the pleasures of the Heart of the Swamp that he forgot about the dangers that lived with him each day and...well, let's just say Alligator had a meal. Now, this was not a strikingly new experience for Geo to witness. He'd seen many others pulled under by Alligator and a few even survive. What made this different was that Able was his best friend, and Geo was working with Able when it happened. After pondering this tragic event, Geo looked to me and asked – for the first time – "Why?"

Dragonfly was excited, for dragonfly is not allowed to guide anyone who does not ask a question. Most in the Heart of the Swamp are so engrossed with the riches and sensuality there that they never stop long enough to ask why, or whether, or what, or how or to question the Heart of the Swamp in any way. Plus, remember the PC Police. I ate 10,000 mosquitoes in 10 minutes and Geo watched in astonishment for he had never seen me behave this way before.

Then, I landed on a branch near Geo's ear and began the long- awaited and joyful task of guiding him out of the Heart of the Swamp. Since I knew Geo loved the sun I began by telling him that there is a place far from the Heart of the Swamp where the sun shines all day and the night sky is full of stars. I cautioned him that the journey out of the Heart of the Swamp was long and that he would need the help and support of others along the way. I explained that we would have to pass through the Backwaters of the Swamp where people live in houses on stilts, and then through the Delta of the Swamp where people cling together so they do not sink into the Shifting Sands. They also cling for fear of getting washed out to sea or back into the Heart of the Swamp by some unseen current or wave. I promised him that if he followed the guidance I gave he would find a sun-drenched place on Rock Solid Ground.

I would be with him throughout the journey, but all I could do was guide him on the right path, directing him around obstacles and pitfalls, eating a few mosquitoes along the way. Geo was a brave young fellow. He agreed to follow me.

We began.

II. The Journey

Getting out of the Heart of the Swamp is not just a matter of wading through the water lilies. Geo had a lifetime of experience going around in circles in the belly of the Heart of the Swamp and was uncomfortable and slightly afraid of straying from the places and sights he had traveled for so long. He was also confused by my instructions that he put aside provisions for the journey since the Heart of the Swamp, he believed, had a never-ending supply of rich, enticing items that he could use for his sustenance. But, setting aside his confusion, doubts, and fears Geo began storing up what he needed for his adventure. Soon he was ready to depart.

As we moved through the murky, water-lily garnished liquid terrain toward the Backwaters, Geo glanced longingly at his lifelong home in the Heart of the Swamp. He began to feel uneasy, anxious, and nostalgic. He had doubts. He worried that where he was headed was more dangerous and less comfortable. He was about to turn back when he noticed unexpected movement ahead. At first it was just a jostling of a few reeds. Then a sight appeared which he'd seen before only on rare occasions. A flat-bottomed boat was

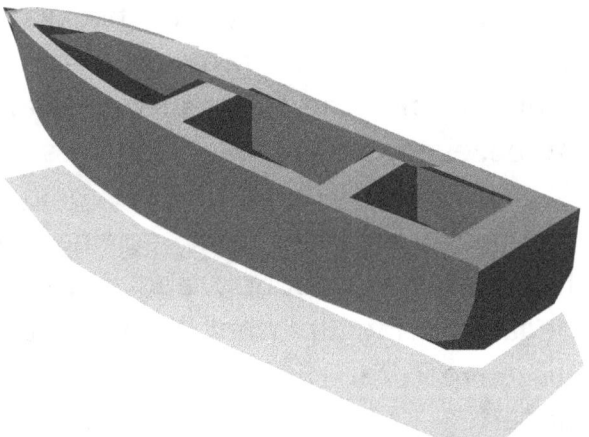

moving quickly and quietly away from the Heart of the Swamp and into the Backwaters. In the boat was a slight person with long, burnished, brown hair who was obviously skilled in rowing and navigating the small watercraft among the moss-drenched trees and omnipresent reeds.

Geo stopped momentarily and stared as the boat disappeared into the Backwaters. I was silent. Geo looked to me for reassurance and perhaps an explanation. I turned without a word and followed the path of the boat into the ever-increasing sunlight that was penetrating the Backwaters. We traveled quite a distance when the boat and its occupant reappeared directly in our path as if out of nowhere.

A series of questions ensued from the Backwater resident in the boat, and I told her of Geo's Quest and our adventure. She seemed a bit confused at first but was open to hearing more. Once she surmised that Geo was no threat she helped him into the boat, and we began an informative trip to her home nestled among the trees and reeds of the Backwaters. Her name was Gea.

Geo quickly discovered the comfort of living in a house.

Gea showed him that he could store food and other supplies so that he was not bound to the never- ending quest for the essentials of living. He found that navigating the Swamp in a flat-bottomed boat allowed him to visit the Heart of the Swamp whenever he wanted without binding him to its unceasing struggle for survival, which he had recognized for the first time. Gea also taught him the mantras of the Backwaters: stay in the boat or in the house; always hide part of your wealth where no one else can find it; don't stray from the ways of the Backwater or you will perish. There were many others.

Geo listened intently and learned quickly. He soon found work in the Backwaters. He and Gea became good friends and partners as he continued to live in Gea's house. However, Geo did not ask any more questions. He was becoming comfortable in the Backwaters and had forgotten the goal we had mutually set of finding his way out of the Swamp to the solid ground where the sun shone and stars lit the night sky. Gea too was content that she had found a partner and helper and that their hidden, saved wealth was growing. Both were becoming complacent.

Were it not for the Storm they may have lived the rest of their lives in the Backwaters. It started as many rainstorms do in the Backwaters: as a gently blowing breeze washing the air with softly flowing raindrops. But this Storm was different. It quickly changed into a ferocious wind that bent giant trees and broke weak branches from weaker trees. It capsized flat-bottomed boats, which forced passengers to grab passing debris in their attempts to reach safety. It tore roofs from houses and destroyed some houses completely, turning them into rubble that was randomly scattered throughout the Backwaters till it was no longer recognizable.

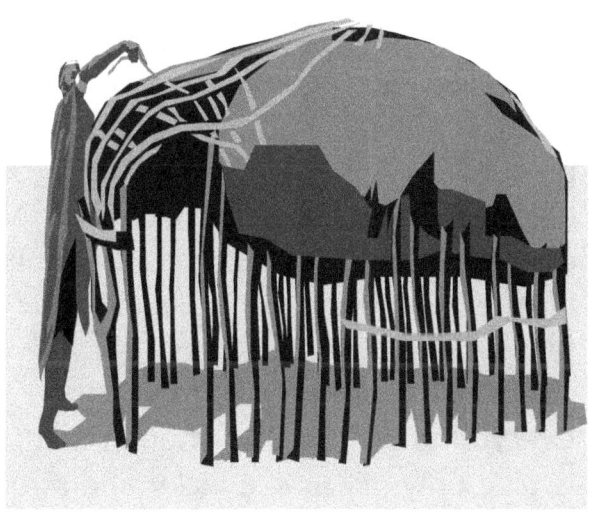

Gea's house was spared the worst of fates, but it was severely damaged when a large branch crashed through the roof and then through the floor into the churning Backwaters. Worse, however, was the damage to the lives of these two young partners, for part of what was lost when the branch invaded their home was their secreted savings stored under the floor of the house. The branch had dislodged their secret savings box and sent it into the turbulent Backwaters, washing it away to some unknown burial plot.

Another crisis had occurred. It prompted Geo to ask me for a second time: "Why?" Dragonfly was again presented with the opportunity to offer guidance to his friend and was delighted even further when Gea joined in the questioning. I explained the fallacy of the Backwaters: that if you recite the mantras and follow the rules everything will be OK, when in fact that is true only if you are lucky and strong. Many who were damaged by the Storm did not lose everything. They said their survival was proof that life in the Backwaters is the only life to live. Some returned to the Heart of the Swamp, broken and disillusioned.

Some few ask "Why?" Fewer still listen to and understand the response. Those few follow their dragonfly out of the Backwaters, through the Delta and to the final, sun-drenched, star-studded destination, Rock Solid Ground.

III. The Quest

Geo and Gea were among the few; those who listened, considered and understood that reciting the mantras and following the rules of the Backwaters, while offering an illusory veil of security, did not promise much more than temporary respite from the arduous life of those benighted souls in the Heart of the Swamp. The Storm was the teacher, and Geo and Gea were willing learners. So, we began preparations. Geo and Gea repaired the damage to the house. They began to accumulate what they needed for their journey and their Quest. When they had what they needed to move forward, they sold the house and most of their belongings. They loaded the boat with essentials and embarked on the voyage that would lead them out of the Backwaters.

Geo and Gea knew that their first opportunity to see the sun filling the entire sky and the stars in all their abundance would be at the fringe of the Swamp, called the Delta. They had learned that those who lived in this part of the Swamp did not believe that they were in the Swamp at all but thought of themselves as liberated from the Swamp. What Geo and Gea had not learned was that the Delta was filled with not only Alligator and Snake, but also with a predator they had not known before: Shark.

They were also unaware that Storm, Wave, and Rushing River continued to be threats to the inhabitants of this most populated place in the Swamp, just as they had been in the Backwaters.

When they first arrived at the Delta, Geo and Gea observed that the inhabitants seemed to cling to each other continually. After living there for a very brief period, the reason became clear when a heavy Wave rolled into the Delta and nearly knocked them over. They narrowly escaped being pulled out to Sea with its undertow.

A nearby denizen grabbed Geo as he was reaching for Gea. They learned quickly that everyone in the Delta stayed close to others to ward off the Shark, to withstand the Wave and the Storm, and to hold each other firm when Rushing River flowed mercilessly through the Delta.

Geo and Gea became comfortable in the Delta very quickly. It was much more open and free than either the Backwaters or the Heart of the Swamp. The PC Police were less visible and forceful. The mantras and rules were less rigid. In addition, since Geo and Gea were both shrewd and ambitious, it was easy to build a cadre of people who would help and support them. They settled in. They knew that this was not the true destination, but it was so much more fun than the Backwaters and so much more pleasant than the

Heart of the Swamp. They began to think they might just stay in the Delta with the many others who had come this far and settled.

After a while, however, Geo and Gea became less enthusiastic. The Shark was nipping at their heels constantly. Alligator was lurking in the rushes, and Snake was always alert for a chance to strike as he slithered through the Shifting Sands, which threatened to swallow anyone who settled in one place too long. Storm was threatening frequently. Rushing River was entirely unpredictable and Wave was incessant. Geo and Gea finally asked the next questions – the questions that would allow me to lead them out of the Swamp and onto Rock Solid Ground.

They wanted to know if life in the Delta was always this stressful. They wanted to know what it would take to wake them up and motivate them to follow the path to Rock Solid Ground. What other disasters might be just around the corner?

Dragonfly's task was almost done.

IV. The Treasure

Like every adventure that leads to a better world, this one doesn't end without a struggle.

Geo and Gea began the preparations to move out of the Delta when Storm and Wave combined to destabilize the entire Delta pushing a great number of people into the Backwaters and the Heart of the Swamp. Alligator and Snake took advantage of the plight of the people and feasted on the weakest. Then Rushing River thundered down on the Delta, and in league with the undertow of Wave washed many out to sea where Shark had his fill.

Geo and Gea were among the blessed. Because they were preparing for their journey and the end of their quest they had begun divesting themselves of the burdens imposed on those living in the Swamp's Delta. Although they didn't escape the devastation entirely, they were able to salvage enough to allow them to begin their final journey to Rock Solid Ground.

Those who remained in the Delta banded together tighter than before and decided to write new rules and to learn the mantras of those who survived with the most – even though it was less than they had before the devastation. They would not listen to or comprehend the words of their dragonfly for they feared that Rock Solid Ground was a myth and that dragonfly was trying to lead them to destruction. They allowed fear to bind them to each other and to the Delta with all of its burdens, stress, and risk.

But Geo and Gea set off. They traveled a long time and found the Delta receding so that Shark and Alligator and Snake could not find their way. The Shifting Sands became more stable, the Wave became a mere ripple, and the Rushing River turned into a gentle stream. They were leaving the Swamp entirely.

And they did. They finally found their way to a place where people lived on Rock Solid Ground. These people had solidly built houses with foundations fortified with fundamentally good materials. These houses had walls that were solid masonry, concrete and stone. Their windows had shutters that were sturdy and that worked when needed, as well as roofs that could withstand the most severe conditions. Geo and Gea couldn't build the house of their dreams at first, but they could buy a small cottage that someone who went before them had outgrown.

And they did. As the years went by they continued to follow the guidance of dragonfly (who continued to eat mosquitoes for them and for their children, Geo Jr. and Gea Jr.). The family built successively larger, more beautiful, and stronger homes for themselves.

They returned to the Heart of the Swamp, to the Backwaters and to the Delta many times to visit friends and to take advantage of the diversity and excitement that was the Swamp's siren song. But

they didn't move in, and they didn't keep a separate residence there. Occasionally one of their friends from the Swamp would ask Geo and Gea about their new life and how to get out of the Swamp. They would tell them to listen to dragonfly…
And some did……..

EPILOGUE

It would be easy to explain the significance of each of the characters in this allegory. That might make it easier for you to grasp the general meaning of the story, but it would not lead you to examine yourself in this tale. Much of what we learn in life comes from examination, inquiry and the insights that derive from that process.

Every character, from the tree that Geo slept in to the solid ground upon which he built his home and the home itself, has meaning. It is obvious that I cast myself in the role of dragonfly, and my clients as Geo and Gea and their offspring. So at least that is settled and gives you a starting point. It is up to you to invest significance in the other characters in the Swamp Story and to discover how that is valuable for you. Some of it will come easily. Other aspects may elude you completely.

Once you feel you have completed your analysis, I would welcome your comments and observations. In exchange for your comments, I will give you mine and perhaps we can find a way to contribute to each other's success and happiness from this dialogue.

One final thought: If you recall, the Introduction started with this quote by Dr. Agon Fly:

"If you do what everyone else does, you'll get the same results they do."

Another famous person said it this way:

"The significant problems we have cannot be solved at the same level of thinking with which we created them." Albert Einstein

Our financial advisors and planners of the late 20th century have not consistently created wealth for us. By following their lead, we have become a society weakened by credit card debt, refinance debt, auto loan debt, even 401k debt, with a savings rate of less than 1%. In fact, the current paradigm has led us into the swamp. Now, there are only a small number of advisors who are even aware that we are in a swamp, with fewer still who know how to get us out of the swamp.

You owe it to yourself to find out if this approach makes sense for you and your family. I encourage you to get your copy of _Money for Life...How to thrive in good times and bad,_ to study it and put what it teaches into practice.
https://www.amazon.com/Money-Life-Thrive-Good-Times/dp/0979770904/ref=sr_1_1?keywords=MONEY+FOR+LIFE+JEFFREY+REEVES&qid=1577417827&s=books&sr=1-1

You will be rewarded with financial security and peace of mind.

www.ingramcontent.com/pod-product-compliance
Lightning Source LLC
Chambersburg PA
CBHW070802220526
45466CB00013B/2072